THE LITTLE
PINK BOOK OF

Etiquette

*A Civilized Person's Guide
to Getting It Right*

RUTH CULLEN

ILLUSTRATED BY KERREN BARBAS

 PETER PAUPER PRESS, INC.
WHITE PLAINS, NEW YORK

*To my exceedingly polite family,
and especially Caroline and Bryce*

Designed by Heather Zschock

Illustrations copyright © 2005 Kerren Barbas

Visit us at www.peterpauper.com

THE LITTLE
PINK BOOK OF

Etiquette

CONTENTS

INTRODUCTION

Do you tell your boss she has spinach in her teeth? Is it ever OK to "curb" your dog on your neighbor's lawn? What do you say to people who ask, "How much do you make?" or, "Are those real?"

Today's etiquette is so much more than keeping elbows off tables or shelving white shoes after Labor Day. It's about remembering the "business" in "business casual." It's resisting the temptation to forward e-mails, USE ALL CAPS—or worse—*emoticons*. It's knowing when to shut off our ever-ringing cell phones!

But even more important, etiquette is about civility—indeed the very foundation of our society. We humans need parameters for our behavior or we become, well, *uncivilized*. Without etiquette, why, we might be raging on roads, cutting the line, and parking in handicapped spaces! We need etiquette now more than ever, before thank you notes and RSVPs go the way of the dinosaur.

Consider *The Little Pink Book of Etiquette* your essential guide to good manners. Chock-full of timely tips and practical advice from A to Z, it will teach you how to handle—and *not* handle—some of today's trickiest etiquette dilemmas.

attitude and everyday etiquette

Civility costs nothing.

PROVERB

ATTITUDE PLATITUDES

Attitude is everything! Positive attitudes are contagious! Smile, and the world smiles back at you!

Well, if truth be told, people really do shine when shone upon, and your good attitude is more than just a sunny disposition—it's good manners.

Here's a newsflash: Etiquette is not about *you*. It's about acting with respect, kindness, and consideration for *others*. It's about empathy. Knowing which fork to use or what to do with a finger bowl may help you at the formal dinner party, but knowing how to make positive connections with others through your positive *out*look—not *in* look—will help you wherever you go.

When casual friends or acquaintances ask, "How are you?" they really don't want to hear a laundry list of complaints or gushing pride about your life. Save these replies for your therapist, family, or very closest friends. Give everyone else a brief, positive response that keeps the conversation moving and focuses on them (e.g., "Great, thanks. And you?"), even if it's not exactly the truth.

The Ten Commandments of Everyday Etiquette

1. Focus on others. It's not about you.
2. Think before you act.
3. Think before you speak.
4. Wait your turn.
5. Listen when others speak.
6. Pick up after yourself.
7. Assist those in need.
8. Respect people who are different from you.
9. Be patient and kind.
10. Smile.

SERVICE WITH A SMILE

What happened to, "Speak with a smile in your voice," or, "The customer is always right"?

Oh, right. Those philosophies got shipped off to India. Sadly, the exponential growth of service industries—restaurants, shopping malls, health care—has occurred at the same time businesses have been downsized, reorganized, outsourced, and off-shored. Now our unwritten mission statements are "Speak with a live person? Ha!" and "The customer can like it or lump it." And it's too bad, really, because whether we work as plumbers, doctors, receptionists, or drugstore clerks, we're all in the service business. And our poor manners and general rudeness are never justified regardless of how challenging our jobs or however many times we've been laid off.

 Don't let bad service taunt you into behaving badly yourself. If you are not satisfied with the service you are receiving, then put on your warmest smile and calmly ask to speak to a supervisor. Find the right person who has the authority to help you, and be specific about what you want (e.g., an apology, a new toaster). If you get nowhere, make sure to document names, ranks, and serial numbers (and specific examples of poor service), and direct your complaint to the corporate office (if applicable). Should they fail to resolve the problem to your satisfaction, take your complaint to the next level, such as your local political representative, a government regulatory department, or the Better Business Bureau. Demand the service you deserve— just be cool, calm, collected, *and mannerly* while you do it.

FAUX PAS:
OOPS, I DID IT AGAIN

You spill red wine on your mother-in-law's white couch. You re-gift last year's hostess gift to the very person who gave it to you. You go to introduce someone, and you blank on their name.

Accidental breaches of etiquette come in many forms, and some cannot be avoided. No one is immune to the occasional social blunder or faux pas, so when they happen, deal with them graciously and always with a sense of humor.

If you forget someone's name at the moment you are to introduce them, then be honest: "I'm terribly sorry but would you please remind me of your name?" If you're particularly savvy, you

might find success in the "Have you met . . . ?" technique. By the count of three, most people will usually introduce themselves, and you escape socially unscathed. (Read more about Introductions on pages 77-85.)

As for spinach in the teeth, toilet paper stuck to shoes, and other potentially embarrassing observations, by all means inform the offender so as to prevent any further embarrassment. But don't confuse faux pas resulting from poor judgment with the accidental varieties. It's never OK to "accidentally" overhear conversations by listening from other phone extensions, or to curb your dog on your neighbor's lawn—even if you clean it up. People may forget your name, but they'll remember how you treated their grass.

bad habits

Giving up smoking is easy . . .
I've done it hundreds of times.

MARK TWAIN

ORAL FIXATIONS AND NERVOUS TICS

Blame it on the caffeine in our triple espresso mocha lattes or the sugar in our "energy" drinks, but we cannot sit still anymore. Even when we try to slow down, our bodies still keep going like engines revving in neutral. And all the foot tapping, knuckle cracking, and nail biting has got to stop!

Gum chewing was prohibited in school for a reason: *it's annoying*. Unless you're a cow, the incessant chewing of anything has no place in public, and especially not in business meetings, lecture halls, and waiting rooms. The same holds true for fidgeting and general restlessness. Feet need not dance while you sit, barring some legitimate medical condition, of course. If they do, it's either time to ixnay on the Tarbucksay, or get thee to a yoga class.

SMOKING: BUTT OUT

Ah, that sexy, sexy cigarette. So sleek and alluring but dangerous with a capital DARN—as in DARN your hair, clothes, and car stink like the Philip Morris building in Marlboro country.

If you choose to smoke, then by all means puff, puff, puff away to your lungs' content. Drive on over to the nicotine station and fill 'er up. Just don't let your good manners go up in smoke when you do.

Heavy smokers (as in people who smoke a lot, not smokers who weigh a lot) may not realize the degree to which their stale cigarette smoke clings to them and the indoor spaces they occupy. If you smoke heavily and know that you will be attending a doctor's appointment or professional meeting, then please try to minimize

your smoking immediately preceding these occasions. Your doctor, her subsequent patients, and everyone who rides the elevator will appreciate the courtesy.

Smoke with wild abandon in the privacy of your own car, but please don't toss cigarette butts from your car window. Smoking can, in fact, be performed with class, and all cars are equipped with ashtrays. Littering out car windows reeks bad manners for many reasons—fire safety for one.

And always be wary of the fact that some people cannot tolerate the smell of your burning cigarette. Before you light up, please pay special mind to your surroundings so that you avoid any small children, pets, people on ventilators, or open fuel tanks.

SLOPPY DRUNKS

Weebles wobble but drunks fall down.

They also spill drinks, vomit, and slur their words, usually while saying something to the effect of, "I love you guys." Sometimes they're downright dangerous, threatening to drive their cars or perform gravity-defying stunts. But despite their impaired states, sloppy drunks deserve the same respect and courtesy you show them when they're sober—albeit with some premeditated trickery.

With safety in mind, you might enlist a co-conspirator to obtain car keys, telephones, or other dangerous items from the inebriated individual. Do whatever it takes—lie, cheat, steal—to ensure that the drunken person does not get behind the wheel of a car. You might not end up winning an Academy Award, but these actions may well be some of the very best manners of all.

ceremonies and
special occasions

*Don't reserve your best behavior for
special occasions. You can't have two sets of
manners, two social codes—one for those you
admire and want to impress, another for
those whom you consider unimportant.*

LILLIAN EICHLER WATSON

HERE COMES THE
BRIDAL SHOWER

*In honor of your upcoming nuptials,
and in celebration of a long and
prosperous married life, I hereby
present you with . . . a Crock-Pot
with matching lingerie.*

Present day wedding showers run the gamut
from champagne brunches to his-and-her
weenie roasts. Often hosted by mothers
or sisters of the bride about one to two
months before the wedding, celebrations of
this nature usually involve food, light-
hearted games about the betrothed couple,
and gifts. Lots and lots of gifts.
Of course, the first rule of
thumb for invitees is to RSVP
promptly.

Bridal showers sometimes
inspire unfortunate lapses of

etiquette. Bridal faux pas include printing gift registry information on the shower invitation, or neglecting to write thank you notes. Guest faux pas include failing to RSVP. When the happy event inspires graciousness and good taste, the bride feels honored by her guests, and vice versa.

HAPPILY EVER AFTER

It may be *your special day*, but your wedding and the events leading up to it would not be nearly as special without the love and support of your families and close friends. The following practical tips will help you keep your etiquette in check and make every day a honeymoon for all involved.

KEEP A RECORD OF GIFTS YOU RECEIVE:

Use a wedding planner book or simple checklist to keep track of gifts, senders, dates received, and whether or not you've sent a thank you note.

THANK YOUR ATTENDANTS WITH GIFTS:

It is traditional to present wedding attendants with a gift to thank them for their participation in your special day. It's also traditional to give a gift to your new spouse, and

 thoughtful to send a gift to both sets of parents the day after the wedding. Traditional gifts include jewelry, or engraved items like pens, jewelry boxes, and picture frames. A handwritten note of thanks to each of your attendants should accompany each gift. An ideal time to present attendants with their gifts is at the rehearsal dinner, when you and your spouse-to-be can publicly state your appreciation.

MAKE THANK YOU NOTES A PRIORITY: Send thank you notes as soon as possible and at least within three months of the wedding. Be specific when acknowledging gifts received, and if you receive gifts of money, you might consider telling the givers how you used their gifts.

INCLUDE THOSE WHO CANNOT ATTEND: Deceased family members or those who cannot attend your wedding for another reason may be acknowledged in a special prayer, or in a speech at the reception. You might also want to carry a keepsake or flower as a reminder.

RECEIVE YOUR GUESTS AND MAKE THE ROUNDS: The bride and groom should personally greet each guest following the wedding ceremony, either through a receiving line or by circulating during their wedding reception. The traditional order of the receiving line places the reception hosts— usually the bride's parents—at the fore, then the groom's parents, the bridal couple, and, if desired, the honor attendants and the rest of the wedding party. When making introductions, you should present a junior person to a senior person (this applies to both age and rank). Also, try to include some helpful information to get a conversation started: "Dad, I'd like you to

meet Sporto Nelson, an expert on acid rain and pretty decent golfer to boot!" (Read more about Introductions on pages 77-85.)

BURNT WEDDING TOASTS

"Normie, as your best man, I mean, what can I say? I love you man! Dude, it's a good thing Annie came along when she did, know what I'm sayin'? You were, like, seriously scraping the bottom of the barrel. Remember that night in Atlantic City? Anyhow, I'm really happy for you guys and hope the new ball-n-chain keeps Normie in line. Just joshing ya, Annie! Cheers! Now I'd like to turn it over to Annie's sister, Lisa."

"Uh, thanks? Well, um, I really just want to say thank you to Norman for revealing a different side to my sister. Who knew that she could be so caring and thoughtful? Maybe it's because of the baby on the way. Oh shoot, was I not supposed to say that? Well, um, anyways, here's to the bride and groom!"

Timeless Tips for Wedding Toasters

- *"Brevity is the soul of wit"; keep it short.*

- *The best toasts may include brief stories, fitting proverbs, and sentimental words about the couple. Appropriate humor works as long as it "toasts," not "roasts."*

- *Plan your speech and rehearse it ahead of time to improve both content and delivery.*

- *Avoid clinking silverware on glassware to get the attention of wedding guests. Simply stand, raise your glass, and repeat the words, "May I please have your attention?" as many times as necessary.*

- *Refrain from excessive celebration (e.g., champagne) before toasting the couple, lest anyone gets singed by inappropriate comments or too personal information. (Also, refer to Sloppy Drunks on page 21.)*

BABY SHOWERS AND CHILDISH GAMES

Baby showers celebrate the imminent arrival of a new baby and provide friends and family the opportunity to "shower" the mother-to-be with practical gifts and advice. But too often shower guests are reduced to playing childish games for the sake of entertainment.

Baby shower guests need not suffer through ridiculous games for the same reason wedding guests should be spared the Chicken Dance. Before you contemplate any party games that require guests to speak in baby-talk, or even consider serving your rum punch in baby bottles with nipple caps, think about the dignity and comfort of your guests. They'll be glad you did.

Baby Showers 101

- *Baby showers are traditionally women-only events hosted by close personal friends of the mother-to-be, but nowadays it is perfectly acceptable for family members to host baby showers, and for celebrations to include fathers-to-be and other male friends and relatives.*

- *Always remember to RSVP when invited.*

- *Baby showers usually take place one to two months before the expected due date, although some women choose to postpone any celebrations until after the baby has arrived.*

- *Appropriate baby shower gifts include practical baby gear (e.g., strollers, car seats, clothing, bottles), as well as personal gifts for the parents-to-be (e.g., gift certificates to to a baby store or spa). Shower guests should ask the hostess if the mother-to-be is registered at a store, and they may choose to purchase a gift from the registry.*

- *To avoid time-consuming activities centered on opening gifts and passing them around, some shower hosts instruct guests to bring unwrapped gifts with their names attached, and then they simply display them at the shower. If gifts are opened at the shower, a list should be kept of who gave what, for later reference in writing thank you notes.*

- *Keep baby shower conversations focused on the excitement of a new baby and the joys of parenthood. Do not share graphic details of your own childbirth experiences, or discuss other people's struggles with infertility, birth defects, or the like.*

FUNERALS:
GRIEVOUS ERRORS

The death of a loved one brings about expressions of sympathy that sometimes exacerbate the pain of the loss. Blunders occur when people either fail to communicate their sympathy at all because they don't know what to say, or they say too much, such as sharing their own tales of woe as a means of assuaging someone else's grief.

But it's never a good idea to share your own horror stories while someone's living their own, or to say anything to the effect of, "I know how you feel" or "Pull yourself together!" Instead, keep your comments brief and focused on the loss at hand: "I'm so sorry. He will be greatly missed." Depending on your relationship to the bereaved, you may offer tangible ways to assist them in the

weeks or months following their loss, such as providing meals, childcare, or other household help. (Read more about Condolence Notes on pages 99-101.)

In addition to personal notes and words of sympathy, other typical condolence offerings include flower arrangements, plants, and donations to a favorite cause or charity made in memory of the deceased. Obituaries and death notices usually indicate the manner in which families wish to honor a loved one. In general, you can't go wrong by wearing conservative, muted-colored clothing when attending funerals, memorial services, or wakes, and keeping any personal visits brief.

And please, "In lieu of flowers" means *no flowers*. Please don't arrive at the funeral home with a huge bouquet—unless you really want to receive the look of death.

children, teenagers, and families

*The hardest job kids face today
is learning good manners
without seeing any.*

FRED ASTAIRE

THE WELL-BEHAVED CHILD

Monkey see. Monkey do.

Despite how many times you try to instill good manners in your offspring, if you model rude, boorish, or unscrupulous behavior, your little ducklings will too. It's a theory called imprinting.

Young children need and want adults to set limits for them, to teach them what it means to exhibit polite behavior so they can become successful and live happily ever after. But too often, our actions contradict our words. "Because I said so" never convinces children not to lie, cheat, or steal if they observe you lying about their age at the amusement park ("He's only five. He's just big for his age."), or eating bunches of grapes while you shop.

Teach your children well by setting a good example, and imprint behaviors that would impress even the likes of Mother Goose.

TOP TIPS FOR TEENS

Being a teenager is hard enough without parents, teachers, and etiquette books always on your back about something or other.

If you're like most teens, though, you understand the direct correlation between pleasing adults and getting what you want. That said, here are some timeless tips to help you get what you want and please others in the process:

DON'T INTERRUPT: It's never a good idea to interrupt adults when they're blathering on and on about "important stuff," so don't. Just nod your head with an interested expression on your face and keep quiet. If you must speak, interject your thoughts without flailing  your arms around or raising your voice (lest your insightful comments get labeled "back-talk" or "sass").

WATCH YOUR BODY LANGUAGE: Adults seem to read into everything, so be careful not to laugh hysterically while looking in their general direction, or do anything "suggestive" like slouching, contorting your face, or exercising your fingers (by snapping them, of course).

NIP THE SLANG: Speak to adults as you would speak to visitors from foreign lands (like Mars). All your clever slang gets lost in translation, so stick to proper English and don't waste your breath trying to explain what "homey" means.

DRESS THE PART: When it comes to special occasions like your bat mitzvah or visiting your mom's workplace, just resign yourself to the fact that you can't wear what you want—especially if you're eyeing the hot pants and halter top in your closet.

HANG UP THE PHONE: Adults have *serious* phone issues, so be sure that you give them their phone messages, ask before you make long distance calls, and never, ever let them see you drop the receiver onto the floor when a call's not for you. Also, forget about making or receiving calls from the dinner table or during the Sunday family outing.

EAT SLOWLY: It's not your fault you've got hungry hormones to feed and they want it as fast as you can shovel it in! But the adults by your side want to eat too, so don't take more than your fair share, or inhale more than you can chew.

SAY THANK YOU: Just because you've said it (three times to be exact), doesn't mean they heard you, so sound off your words of thanks in a card or note whenever you receive a gift. Writing thank you notes shows people you care, and acknowledges them for their thoughtfulness. So don't hesitate, even if the gift you received was incredibly lame, and even if you're away at school or summer camp. Just write the thank you note. And you can rest assured you'll have plenty more gifts heading your way.

Ex Marks the Spot

After a break-up, the way you deal with your ex puts your manners on full display. You can either rise like the cream in your coffee, or sink like the sand-bag you tied to your ex's golf clubs.

There's no excuse for rude or disrespectful behavior, particularly when kids are involved. The worst thing you can do is hurl insults and half-eaten pretzels at one another while attending junior's soccer game. No matter if *she* started it, or *he* brought his new girlfriend, or *she* said this, or *he* did that.

If you cannot stomach your ex's presence, then steer clear of activities in which encounters are likely. But since this is not always possible (e.g., at your child's wedding), you must find ways to cope that do not involve narcotics or childish games ("I can't see you. I can't hear you.").

In the event your ex dies, you might be surprised to find yourself stricken with mixed emotions, regardless of how long you've been apart or despite any additional spouses (think: Cher's very public reaction to Sonny Bono's untimely death). Pay respect to your ex with respect for others, such as children and new spouses. And if you are asked to speak on your ex's behalf, do so only if you have nice things to say, of course.

UNDER ONE ROOF WITH ROOMMATES AND FAMILIES

Billie Holiday isn't the only one singing the blues. At all hours of the day and night, you can hear your roommates and family members belting out such favorites as, "Dirty, Dirty Dishes," "Trail o' Wet Towels," and "She's Got My Remote."

After a brief honeymoon period with a new roommate, spouse, or child, things can get ugly—and fast. We're talking apple cores on coffee tables, toilet seats left up, hair in the  shower drain, and spilled orange juice in the refrigerator. Although we may say, "Don't wear my Sponge Bob watch unless you *ask me* first!" what we're really saying is, "Show me some courtesy and respect."

We exhibit courtesy and respect on the home front by paying attention to how our actions affect those around us. If you don't think anyone really cares about your table crumbs or the fact that you borrow their toothbrush "only occasionally," try not flushing for a day or two and watch how fast your roommates sprout horns.

It's these very devilish details that send people over the edge—usually while they're mumbling something about toothpaste caps or dirty laundry. Keep the peace in your home by starting small (e.g., shutting drawers you open, cleaning up messes you make), and working your way up to larger things (e.g., vacuuming, assisting with meal preparation and clean-up). Show your love—and good manners—with your actions, and soon everyone will be singing "Hallelujah!"

dating

*Courtesy is as much a mark of
a gentleman as courage.*

THEODORE ROOSEVELT

Uh, Yeah.
I'll Call You.

Dating is much like interviewing for a job. You clean yourself up, put your charming, witty self on display, and then wait for something to happen. And your good manners can make all the difference when it comes to scoring the job or second date.

The foremost rule of dating concerns cold, hard cash. As a general rule, the person who asks for the date pays for the date. Although you may wish to split the bill by choice, as someone else's date you are not required to do so.

When the date is underway, do not ask for doggie bags, talk about exes, or receive cell phone calls—especially on first dates. You'll have plenty of opportunities

later in the relationship to ignore your companion and make a pig of yourself. (Refer to Exes on pages 42-43 and read more about Phones on pages 55-60.)

Now here's the tricky part. Though convenient and tempting, it's never a good idea to say you'll call or e-mail when you know you won't. When possible, be direct so that you avoid setting false expectations for someone else. Mature or direct types may have no trouble calling it like they see it: "Though I don't think we're a match, Tito, I enjoyed meeting you and wish you all the best. Buh bye." More times than not, however, our actions speak louder than our words. It may seem rude or cowardly, but when you don't have the heart to tell someone how you really feel ("I can't get past your mullet."), and you try to spare their feelings by hoping they get the message some other way (you move to Toledo), you're actually showing them courtesy and respect. (Refer to White Lies on pages 105-06.)

If they don't read your signals (you're never home, or you're very busy, or you have malaria, or the like) then give them time. If they're still calling two years later and lurking outside your workplace, then call the police.

PDA:
Kindly Get a Room

Some expressions of love or attraction simply don't belong in the public eye—such as when your Labrador retriever mounts your neighbor's leg at the annual May Day celebration. Indeed, observing very public displays of affection, or PDA, beyond the occasional holding of hands or kiss on the cheek, may find you yelling, "May Day!"

Love may be a many splendored thing, but PDA should be a many censored thing. In the minds of well-mannered people around the world, it already is. Exercise some restraint and respect for those around you, and keep your displays of affection behind closed doors.

electronic etiquette

*Etiquette means behaving
yourself a little better than
is absolutely essential.*

WILL CUPPY

FLAMING E-MAILS AND EXPLOSIVE BLOGS

Once upon a time, long before telephones, text messaging, and e-mail, people communicated by writing letters. Letter writers scribbled out their deepest thoughts—their hopes, fears, and dreams—crumpling paper after paper until they got it just right.

Modern day advances allow us to fire off communications with lightning speed, and post diaries of our most intimate thoughts online. But convenience has a price.

In haste, fury, or just plain laziness, we blast off correspondence rife with spelling and grammatical errors, and charged with way too much emotion. We SHOUT our words in all caps, punctuate sentences with emoticons (:-o), and imitate the likes of e e cummings by failing to use punctuation or capitalization at all.

We simply forget the power of the written word, and the fact that our e-mails, websites, and blogs become public knowledge the instant we hit the "send" key.

Before you inadvertently "flame" your boss, or otherwise write something you wouldn't dare say in public, remember that bad manners are magnified online. So keep yours in check with spell-check, good judgment, and "delete."

GREAT! ANOTHER FORWARDED CHAIN E-MAIL!

Please forward this e-mail to everyone in your address book and you will have good luck forever!

And they will have clogged inboxes, pop-up windows, and disabling computer viruses. Show some respect (and good taste) by making the occasional forwarded joke, picture, or video clip the exception, not the rule. And don't even consider sharing offensive subject matter—especially that of the crude, political, or religious variety.

Am I on Speakerphone?

Although practice usually makes perfect, our telephone manners leave much to be desired. And despite all the options on our phones, it appears we have forgotten how to deliver the basic service.

When answering a ringing phone, the correct response is, "Hello" and "May I ask who is calling?" should callers not provide a name (as they should).

When using services as inherently rude as "call waiting," do not leave one caller on terminal hold in order to speak with someone else. Show respect to caller #1 by either ignoring the incoming call, or quickly disposing of caller #2. However, if you are expecting another call and someone else calls at that time, then take the call but explain your need to interrupt or end the conversation should your other call take place.

Kids and phones rarely mix, so think twice before having your toddler be your receptionist. Also avoid activities like eating, toothbrushing, watching TV, or driving while talking on the phone. Much like operating a chainsaw, good telephone etiquette requires us to pay attention to the task at hand.

And as for speaker phones, bear in mind that many people fear public speaking worse than death itself. Ask for permission before you put someone on speakerphone, and certainly if other people are present.

YELL PHONES

Ringing soon in a theater near you:
Attack of the Killer Cell Phones

Cell phones have invaded all right, and no place is sacred—certainly not libraries, elevators, bathroom stalls, and places of worship.

We chit-chat on cell phones with utter disregard for time and place. Even when we stand before cashiers, doctors, or law enforcement, we hold up a finger as if to say, "One moment, please" while we make dinner reservations or scream, "Can you hear me nowwww?"

What we fail to realize is that cell phones are not people. While it's perfectly acceptable to speak quietly with a companion while waiting in line at the bank, it's not the time to call your friend, Lida, in Arizona. And no one wants to hear you talk to your gynecologist, break up with your boyfriend, or espouse your political views.

Cell phones save the day when you're late for an appointment or your car breaks down. But more times than not, the manner in which we use them disturbs the peace in ways that are truly criminal (assault with a deadly weapon?).

Do your part for World Peace. Help stop the insanity of cell phone misuse by hitting the "off" button, and encourage others to do the same.

LEAVE A SOLILOQUY
AFTER THE BEEP

People have your number all right,
and most of the time it's the digit that
stands for "delete."

Call-answering systems have become far
more sophisticated than most of us realize,
now allowing callers to re-record the messages they leave. (Bet you wish you knew
that before you left that stammering, nervous job inquiry message at the company of
your dreams.)

Regardless, a successful call-back message
need only require a few things: your name,
the purpose of your call (in 10 words or
fewer), and a number where you can be
reached. Speak slowly, and neither shout nor
mumble your words.

Outgoing voicemail or answering
machine messages should also be brief and

sparing in the details. Do not provide too much revealing information (e.g., "We're vacationing in China." "The *love* doctor isn't in right now."), or otherwise greet callers in an unprofessional manner. You never know who might be calling, so save your Donald Duck impression for the one-on-one.

gifts, guests, and entertaining

To be a successful hostess, when guests arrive say, "At last!" and when they leave say, "So soon!"

UNKNOWN

COME ON OVER TO MY PLACE

Martha Stewart's real crime was that she never told us how difficult entertaining really is. She made it all look so darn easy—whipping up soufflés, embroidering pillows, baking bread from wheat that she grew and harvested herself.

But the most skillful hosts and hostesses need not *do it all* to become true domestic divas; they simply need to get organized. Good organization lowers stress, and low stress makes for happy, gracious hosts and hostesses.

Days and even weeks before the party, they finalize menus, prepare serving dishes and utensils, and tend to all the dirty work. By the time their parties begin, they have little else to do but welcome their guests, cater to their needs, and enjoy the atmosphere. And when things go wrong, as they sometimes do (the wine spills, the roast burns), they simply brush it off and call for pizza, without batting an eyelash or losing sight of what's most important—*their guests*.

You, too, can be a host or hostess with the most or mostess. All it takes is some multi-tiered planning, elbow grease, and follow-through. If nothing else, remember that entertaining, like etiquette itself, is not about you; it's about your guests. Focus on their comfort and well-being, and your parties are sure to please.

Entertaining Tips for Hostesses and Guests

- *Use a checklist to guide your preparation before entertaining dinner or overnight guests, and do as much as you can before your guests arrive.*

- *Ask about any food or pet allergies before guests visit, and make plans accordingly.*

- *When you're the guest, arrive at the expected hour and bring a gift for the hostess that suits her tastes or interests (e.g., a bottle of good gin and some fancy olives; a personalized hand towel and new golf tees).*

- *Hostesses should personally greet guests when they arrive, and make them comfortable by taking their coats (if applicable), offering them a drink, and making* introductions to other guests. (Read about Introductions on pages 77-85.)

- At dinner parties where seating has not been pre-arranged with place cards, guests should ask the hostess if she has a preference for the seating arrangement. If not, try to alternate male and female guests at the table, and avoid sitting next to your spouse or companion. Reserve the ends of the table for the host and hostess, or guest of honor (if applicable).

- Do not start eating until the hostess is seated and ready to eat, unless she has specifically instructed you otherwise.

- Pass condiments and food around the table in one direction, and take small portions to ensure enough for all guests. (Read more about Table Manners on pages 134-43.) Hostesses should beware foisting unwanted second and third portions on their guests, just as guests should beware foisting wanted third and fourth portions on themselves.

- At the meal's conclusion, both men and women should offer to assist the hostess with cleanup—although many hostesses prefer to tackle the dishes after the guests have left.

- Guests should not overstay their welcome or otherwise take advantage of the graciousness of the hostess (e.g., asking her to put on a third pot of coffee). Be mindful of context clues such as other guests leaving, or the hostess changing into her nightgown, and thank your hostess while departing at a decent hour.

OVERNIGHT GUESTS

Fish and visitors stink after three days.

BENJAMIN FRANKLIN

When we host overnight guests, as a courtesy we try to make them feel welcome and provide all the creature comforts of home. Unfortunately, sometimes we do such a good job that guests get a little too comfortable, and tensions mount when they unknowingly invade personal space or otherwise cross the line.

To keep expectations in check and pave the way for a successful visit, guests should remember that they are, in fact, guests. This means no feet on the furniture, and no rummaging through refrigerators, drawers, or computer hard drives. As a general rule, guests should pick up after

themselves, wake up at a reasonable hour, and offer to help out with meals and cleanup.

Hosts can do their part by providing guests with a basic agenda for the visit, and communicating some ground rules for their home (e.g., no karaoke before 9:00 AM; help yourself to coffee and bagels if you wake up first). They should also provide amenities such as towels and toiletries, as well as the use of the washing machine and dryer.

Party Crashers and Uninvited Guests

In this age of fleeting logic and absent RSVPs, hosts often find themselves face to face with uninvited or unexpected guests. Surprise!

If you are so inclined, welcome these party crashers and disregard the error of their ways. Indeed, the error might be yours, in that you forgot they were coming or otherwise failed to receive their message. ("Thanks a lot, honey!")

But if you simply cannot accommodate or tolerate their presence, then ever so politely tell them they must leave. Enlist reinforcements if necessary, but do not allow party crashers and uninvited guests to spoil your fun.

A PRESENT? FOR ME?

The best gifts come in small packages. And large packages. And every size package in between.

 We love giving gifts almost as much as we love to receive them. But as we well know, no good deed goes unpunished. When is the last time you wrote a thank you note for a gift? Phone calls and e-mails simply don't cut it when it comes to acknowledging someone's thoughtfulness and generosity. These days, the handwritten thank you note is worth your weight in gold (and that's a lot of gold).

Select gifts with the recipient in mind, especially if you choose to re-gift something you have received. Etiquette mavens are divided on the issue of re-gifting, making it a personal decision. Some condone it, but with caveats: that non-returnable items must be acceptable, that the gift must be appropriate and unused, that the original gift giver will not find out. On this last point, however, some feel the re-gift must be acknowledged to both parties, and a personally chosen gift may be added. (*"Shelly gave me this espresso maker, but since I have two already and you've been wanting one, she thought it would be fine if I passed it on to you. And here are your favorite fair trade shade-grown Sumatran decaf beans I picked up at the café you love so much."*)

Never feel obligated to give someone a gift just because they've given one to you. But if you've been invited to a birthday party or wedding, you should always send a gift even if you can't attend the event.

grammar and language

*Morals and manners
will rise or decline with our
attention to grammar.*

JASON CHAMBERLAIN

SPEAKING LIKE AN AMERICAN

Forget English. Americans speak *American*—a language as colorful and flawed as we are ourselves.

In the name of self-expression, we bend the rules or smash them to smithereens. The result? Spanglish; Hip Hop-ish; Dude-ish (think: surfer and skateboarder lingo); and, Slurrish (think: Anna Nicole Smith)—to name a few.

Most of the time, regardless of our regional, cultural, or socioeconomic backgrounds, we can figure out what the other person is trying to say. But not always, and especially when old words have been assigned new meanings (e.g., "That outfit is *bad!*").

When it comes to etiquette, we must speak a common language so that our good intentions and consideration for others can be understood. Don't confuse Grandma by thanking her for "the bread" when you mean "money," and whatever you do, don't tell her she's "kickin'."

Languages grow and change as we do, but not quite as fast. "Please," "Thank you," "May I...," and "Excuse me" are magic words in any language. Use them.

Common Grammar Pitfalls

- When subjects and verbs don't agree (e.g,. "The cat play with his toy mouse.")

- Ending sentences in a preposition (e.g., "Where are you at?")

- Making up words (e.g., "irregardless")

- Using slang to excess (e.g., "dude," "uh huh," "yeah")

- Developing annoying speech habits ("like," "for real," "know what I'm sayin'")

SLANGUAGE

"Wassup, dawg! You just chillin' at your crib? Gimme a shout later, a'ight? Out."

Translation: *What is up, friend? Are you just relaxing at your house? Give me a call later, all right? Goodbye.*

Slang terms serve a distinct purpose in any society: they foster bonds between like-minded individuals and allow for creative and personalized linguistic expression. While there's nothing wrong with using slang terms with your friends, there's everything wrong with using incomprehensible or obscene language with your boss. So mind your "Peace out's" and "Cool's," and err on the side of proper English.

greetings and introductions

*Anyone can be polite to
a king. It takes a gentleman
to be polite to a beggar.*

UNKNOWN

How *You* Doin'?

Introductions serve to acknowledge others and get the conversation started. But many people fail at introductions by not making them at all. Daunted by social scenarios or uncertain of the rules, people do nothing and feelings get hurt.

Introductions need not be so elusive if we remember some basic guidelines:

- Younger, lower-ranking people and men should be presented *to* older, higher-ranking people and women by first saying the latter's names: "Dad, I'd like to introduce my boyfriend, Slick"; "Mr. President, I'd like to introduce Bubba Jones from the mail room"; "Emily, I'd like you to meet Roland Christopher."

- In casual settings, use full

names when introducing people ("Geneva, this is William Smith. William, this is Geneva Hobart."); and in formal settings, use courtesy titles and last names ("Dr. Hobart, I'd like to introduce my college roommate, Mr. Smith.")

● When introducing family members who share your surname, use first names only ("Please allow me to introduce my husband, Buzz, and our children, Adelaide and Rupert.")

Upon being introduced, a simple, "It's nice to meet you" will do. Wait for others to offer nicknames before you call Elizabeth "Liz," and nip mispronunciations or wrong names in the bud: "The name's Jay, not Alan."

Above all, make an effort to recognize others with courtesy and respect—even if you forget the rules or a name.

I'VE GOT MY EYES ON YOU

In this country, unlike some Asian and Middle Eastern countries, making eye contact while speaking is considered good manners. When we look people in the eyes, we give them our full attention and show them we care.

Good eye contact does not mean staring, which can be creepy or even threatening. Stare a dog in the eyes and risk getting mauled. The same holds true with people. That said, shifty eyes or over-the-shoulder glances disrespect the speaker and may lead to conclusions about the listener: nervous, untrustworthy, *rude*.

Make eye contact by looking people in the eye, and periodical-ly shifting your focus elsewhere. Should the speaker have one lazy eye, multiple piercings, or some other facial distraction, the listener may safely focus his vision on the bridge of the speaker's nose.

PERSONAL SPACE: PLEASE DON'T STAND SO CLOSE TO ME

We may not mark our territories like arctic wolves, but when someone invades our personal space, the fur can really start to fly.

What you consider "friendly distance" may be "too close for comfort" for someone else. If you continually sense that people are backing away from you when you speak, either you've overstepped your bounds, or it's time to lay off the garlic.

Respect the personal boundaries of those around you and pay attention to context clues like facial expressions and body language. It's not OK to place your hands on someone's wheelchair without asking first, nor should you crowd people at the ATM, or conduct loud phone conversations while in close proximity to others.

People leave their DNA on such personal items as car stereo buttons, remote controls, and computer keyboards for a reason, so Do Not Approach unless welcomed to do so.

LET'S SHAKE ON IT

Politicians know better than most the importance of a good, firm handshake.

Done correctly—not too firm, not too limp—and always with the right hand (barring physical disability, of course), handshakes can mean anything from, "Pleasure to meet you" to "You have my word."

What you don't want your handshake to say is, "I am sweaty and nervous." Should you suffer from excessively sweaty palms, visit your local sports retailer and purchase a bottle of gel or powder specifically designed for sweaty palms (tip: check the golf or tennis sections). Otherwise, hit the  "powder room" before you meet and greet, and prepare palms for action with a sprinkle of talcum powder.

Two-handed handshakes, or handshake-half hug combinations, are best reserved for close friends and family. Even then, beware holding on too long lest your handshake say, "I just can't let you go."

COME GIVE YOUR AUNT LIBBY A SMOOCH

Pucker up, because everybody's looking for a kiss nowadays—and especially, it seems, during flu season.

Take your pick. You've got the ever popular air kiss, a fleeting marriage of right cheeks and a kiss to the air. Then there's the one-kisser to the right cheek, or the très European two-kisser to both cheeks—right, then left. Lip locks are usually reserved for lovers or close family members. Aristocratic (or pretentious) types might present the top of a hand. (Refer to Public Displays of Affection on page 50.)

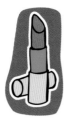 But just because everyone else is kissing doesn't mean you should too. Never feel obligated to say hello with a smooch. If you're suffering from a cold or

just don't wish to get that close, then it's perfectly OK to keep your distance while
extending a hand—to shake, not to kiss.

jobs and careers

*A graceful and pleasing
figure is a perpetual letter
of recommendation.*

FRANCIS BACON

FIRST IMPRESSIONS AND LASTING IMPRESSIONS

Job interviews may last anywhere from fifteen minutes to two hours, but the true test takes place in the first five minutes.

As you enter the room and sit down, your body language and appearance reflect your confidence, attention to detail, and professionalism. If you arrive at an interview armed with qualifications but cloaked in sequins or powder from a jelly donut, your intelligent repartee may fall upon deaf ears. The way you greet your interviewer—nice firm handshake, good eye contact, warm smile—can either project you forward or stop you dead in your tracks.

Focus on the nonverbal messages you send with

the same vigor you apply to answering the interview questions themselves. Should something go wrong such as a wardrobe malfunction or weather delay, handle it with a smile and light-hearted comment, then focus on the business at hand. Your grace-underfire will speak louder than any long-winded excuse.

And be sure to send a thank you note to your interviewers for their time and consideration. A good first impression will get the conversation started, but a good lasting impression will get you the job.

CUBICLE HOPPING AND OFFICE NO-NO'S

Somewhere between new employee orientation and retirement, it happens. We relax.

We get so comfortable in our offices and friendly with our colleagues that we forget we're at work. Faster than you can say "Per your memo about thinking outside the box on that action item," we've got our feet up on the desk so we can touch up our pedicures. We think nothing of sharing details about our impending divorces or cosmetic surgery while we flit in and out of cubicles armed with juicy tidbits from the office rumor mill.

For the record, professional office behavior does not involve chewing the fat with co-workers, let alone gum or tobacco, while you read other people's faxes and shop online. Just because it's "Casual Day" does not mean you can wear a tube top to the office. And it's never OK to pad expense reports, pilfer office supplies, or make long-distance personal calls—even if your boss is a jerk.

To that end, although it's tempting to milk your colleagues for charitable donations, school fundraisers, or otherwise "pass the hat" for gifts and the like, it's not appreciated and certainly not good manners. People come to work to earn money, not to support your child's swim team or bankroll the reception-ist's baby shower. Don't put anyone in the awkward position of feeling obligated to con-tribute to your personal causes. Keep your personal matters to yourself, and work while you're at work.

HEY BOSS, IS THAT MISTLETOE?

"Wow. Charles from Legal sure can moonwalk! And check out Edna from Finance. Talk about assets!"

Before you make grievous errors in judgment at your office holiday party and plunge headfirst into the punch bowl, remember that you're still at work. Though it's called a "party," it's really a test. Don't think for a moment that your drunken antics or sheer blouse will be forgotten when your annual review rolls around and you ask for a raise.

Pass the holiday test by not crossing the line. It is possible to be festive while staying within the bounds of professionalism. And for the sake of your career and general well-being, don't overdo it on the spiked eggnog or make a pass at your boss's spouse.

LOVE AT THE OFFICE

Danger: You are Entering an Office with Dating Co-Workers. Body Armor is Required.

Nothing spells trouble like fraternization between co-workers. Granted, office romances can be very entertaining to watch. What could be more fun than watching lovers quarrel by the copy machine, or ogle each other at the weekly meeting?

But if you're serious about your job and career, you'll keep your love life separate from

your work life. People behave badly when personal and professional lines blur. And once those barriers have been broken, it's nearly impossible to go back to prescribed "codes of conduct." Can you say sexual harassment?

Be kind and respectful to your colleagues, but don't date them. When you do, however, be discreet and make every effort to keep your personal and professional lives separate. The more serious the relationship, the more serious one of you should get about looking for a new job.

letters and notes

*Courtesies of a small and trivial
character are the ones which
strike deepest in the grateful
and appreciating heart.*

HENRY CLAY

I Quit!

Etiquette requires a certain degree of restraint, and the best time to exercise such restraint is when writing a resignation letter for a job you detest. You just never know when that horrid boss may resurface in your life—and rest assured she will—so bite your tongue no matter how justified you might be.

As with all business correspondence, resignation letters should be typewritten in standard business letter format, and directed to a person—in this case your immediate supervisor, with a copy to Human Resources (if applicable). Always state your intention to resign, reason for leaving, and last day of work. Keep letters positive and concise, and, as a courtesy, provide at least two weeks notice. Here's a sample format that is appropriate to use:

Your Address

Today's Date

Employer's Address

Dear (Name of Supervisor):

Please accept my resignation effective two weeks from today, (date).

I have learned much during my (length of employment, i.e. three months/three years) at (name of employer), but have accepted another opportunity to further my career.

Yours Sincerely,

[Your Signature]

Your Full Name
cc. Human Resources

THANK YOU! THANK YOU! THANK YOU!

Hello dear. Since I haven't heard from you in three months, I wondered if you ever received my gift.

If you do nothing else in this life, make it your mission to acknowledge other people's kind deeds with a card or note. When someone does something nice for you, such as holding a door or passing the mashed potatoes, you *say* "thank you." But when they give you a gift, lend you their beach house, or otherwise show you extraordinary kindness or generosity, you *write a thank you note*. You don't even need a reason ("Thanks for being you.").

Write thank you notes promptly and from the heart, using specific language that

recognizes the gift or deed. And don't delude yourself by thinking that pre-printed messages or e-mails carry the same weight as personal letters of thanks—they don't. Above all, even if it's a year late, just write the darn note! Keep it simple and sweet:

Today's Date

Dear Barbara,

Thank you for the enlightening book about shore birds of New England. It will be most helpful when I go birding in Newport this summer.

I appreciate your thoughtfulness. Please send my regards to Reuben!

Sincerely,
Tess

Condolence Notes

Condolence notes should be sent as soon as possible following the death of a friend, acquaintance, or family member. Though shock and sadness often render people speechless during times of grief, even a short note of sympathy to a widow, widower, or close family member will acknowledge their loss and show your support—even if it arrives weeks after the death. If possible, the person receiving a letter of condolence should acknowledge the note in some way, if only with a printed card or a short personal message.

When you write a note of sympathy, you should express your sorrow and if you are close with the bereaved, extend a general or specific offer to help out in some way (e.g., running errands, providing meals, etc.). You may also wish to include some warm or witty anecdote about the deceased: *Just thinking about Arthur's Jerry Lewis impression makes me smile.*

Sample note for
friend or relation:

Today's Date

Dear Penelope,

We were terribly saddened to hear of Sebastian's death. Please know that Charles and I are here for you in any way, and do hope you will let us know if we can help out with the dogs, shopping, or anything else.

You are in our thoughts and prayers.

With deepest sympathy,
Eloise and Charles

making conversation

*We are born charming, fresh
and spontaneous and must
be civilized before we are fit to
participate in society.*

JUDITH MARTIN

ENOUGH ABOUT ME. WHAT DO YOU THINK ABOUT ME?

Leaders are born; conversationalists are made. And learning how to make polite conversation is as easy as turning on your TV.

Certain "news" anchors and political pundits can teach you exactly what not to do when speaking with others: interrupt, fail to listen, dominate the conversation with your own opinions, and look away from the person to whom you are speaking. Sitcoms can illustrate just how agonizing it is to be cornered at a party by a whiner, braggart, or bore.

Talk-show hosts, on the other hand, succeed in engaging their guests in conversation by asking the

right questions. And so can you. When someone new approaches you in a social setting, stand up (if possible), introduce yourself, and use open-ended questioning (e.g., questions with more than one word answers) to get the conversation started. Instead of saying, "Have you tried the hummus?" ask, "How do you know the host?" or, "Did you happen to see that fascinating article about endangered sea turtles in today's *New York Times*?"

People love to talk about themselves, so let them. Just remember not to get too personal or too deep with your questions.

And remember: flattery will get you everywhere, if it's sincere: "Your necklace is stunning!" "Great tie. Not many men can wear that color, but it looks fabulous on you!"

WHITE LIES:
NO, THOSE PANTS DON'T
MAKE YOU LOOK FAT

President George Washington, a.k.a. Mr. "I cannot tell a lie," had it all wrong. In fact, studies now show that kids who are able to tell lies effectively are more successful when it comes to getting along with others.

See Johnny lie. See Johnny have many friends.

Of course, it all depends on the nature of the lie. "White lies" are false or misleading statements made in consideration for others' feelings. (e.g., "I'm sure no one noticed the 'kick me' sign on your back, Theodore." "Your nose isn't too big; it's *distinguished*.")

White lies assist the well-mannered in handling some of life's more difficult scenarios with grace and aplomb. Unlike bold-faced lies made for purely selfish reasons, white lies can enable you to get your point across without crushing someone's heart or ego: "Thanks for the offer, Edward. While the monster truck rally sounds intriguing, I have already made other plans."

Just go easy on the lying, however. Sometimes the truth hurts, and what you say may not make you popular, but it's the best option of all.

COMPLIMENTS:
YOU LOOK MAHVELOUS

Congratulations on passing your medical boards! No one thought you could do it.

Like jokes, compliments are all in the delivery. Specific praise and well-chosen words can make people feel good about some facet of their personality or appearance, or recognize a job well done: "Great job on the Jefferson case, Dave. Your quick thinking really saved the day."

But compliments can have the opposite effect—often unintentionally—when linked with back-handed digs: "Oh Julie, your new dress looks fabulous! It's so much better than that dreadful frock you wore last year."

Worse yet may be empty flattery ("You're hot!"), or

effusive, generic compliments that really mean nothing at all ("Nice outfit, Madelyn. But all your outfits are nice. And so are you. Nice, nice, nice.").

When someone pays you a compliment, accept it graciously by smiling and saying, "Thank you." You will not be deemed snobbish or conceited for doing so; just the picture of exemplary manners.

How Not to Accept a Compliment

- *Make a contorted facial expression.*
- *Roll your eyes.*
- *Say, "You've got to be kidding me!"*
- *Say, "Puh-leeeeeze!"*
- *Say, "No, stop. I hate my hair!"*

QUESTIONS YOU SHOULDN'T ASK

When are you due? How much did that cost? Who'd you vote for? Dating anyone? Are those real???

What a calamity. So many people suffering, no relief in sight. The culprit? Foot-in-mouth disease, a disorder in which the filtering device between the brain and tongue slowly disintegrates, and victims are rendered incapable of preventing fleeting thoughts from leaving their mouths.

No matter where they are, they blurt out whatever's on their mind, including questions that should never be asked: "How old are you?" "Have you gained weight?" "Is that a birthmark or did someone hit you?"

When dealing with people

clearly suffering from this disease, arm yourself with some questions of your own: "Why do you ask?" or, "That's a little personal, don't you think?" Other effective retorts include, "Wouldn't *you* like to know," or "I'll forgive you for asking if you forgive me for not answering."

Regardless of how relentless or bold their attacks, hold your ground and remember that these people are clueless; they know not what they do.

HUMOR: HAVE I GOT A JOKE FOR YOU

So this guy walks into a bar. It hurt.

When it comes to humor, one man's pleasure is another man's pain. Subject matter that you find hilarious might be totally inappropriate or downright offensive to someone else. Use your excellent sense of humor to make other people smile, and fight the urge to tell jokes about politics, race, religion, and sex. Your reputation depends on it.

How Not to be Funny

- *Tell offensive jokes.*

- *Take yourself too seriously.*

- *Dish dirt about other people.*

- *Make fun of people around you in a mean way.*

manners miscellany

The great secret . . . is not having bad manners or good manners or any other particular sort of manners, but having the same manner for all human souls . . .

GEORGE BERNARD SHAW

BORROWING: I'LL GLADLY PAY YOU TUESDAY FOR A HAMBURGER TODAY

Thank goodness for friends and family. Unlike auto dealerships and banks, their deals are often too good to refuse. Need a car for a few days? Just call Uncle Michael. Some quick cash? Ask Dad. Looking for the perfect outfit? A snow blower? A Belgian waffle iron? No problem.

If you play your cards right, a world of goods and riches can be yours by simply asking, "May I borrow that?" But unfortunately, we Americans haven't quite mastered the concept of borrowing. Why else would credit card companies be so willing to offer us thousands of dollars every day of the week?

Borrowing from friends and family is no different than borrowing from anyone else. To borrow is to promise to return whatever it is you have borrowed—with interest (if applicable), in a timely manner, and in the same condition in which you received it.

Should the borrowed item get damaged or lost, then it is the responsibility of the borrower to make up for the loss. What could be more simple? Now, can I borrow that?

Timeless Tips for Borrowers

- *Establish a timeframe when you borrow something, and respect it.*

- *Return borrowed items in the same condition in which you received them.*

- *Replace borrowed items if you lose or damage someone else's property.*

- *Avoid borrowing personal items that are impossible to replace.*

- *If you find yourself borrowing the same thing repeatedly, go out and buy one for yourself.*

HOSPITAL VISITS

Code Blue. First Floor. We've got an urgent need for some first aid in the etiquette department.

People are admitted to hospitals because they require specialized medical care. Oftentimes, they are sick, in pain, and do not feel well. Once admitted, hospitalized patients are given a room—sometimes with roommates—and subjected to flimsy night-gowns, sleep interruptions, and lots of poking and prodding.

For safety reasons, most hospitals strictly forbid visitors from bringing certain items such as latex balloons or flowers into their facilities. People with allergies or compromised immune systems can suffer life-threatening reactions to pollen

from floral arrangements, or even to strong odors from perfumes, aftershaves, and scented lotions.

Before you drop in on an ailing friend or relative in the hospital, always call first to make sure your visit is welcome. If so, then prepare for your visit by *toning it down*. This means going easy on fragrance, keeping your voice quiet, and respecting the other patients and hospital staff you will encounter. Keep your visits brief, and ask the patient if there is anything you can do or get for him or her (e.g., water the plants at home, buy reading material, etc.).

But unless you are a very close friend or family member, you should forgo hospital visits and send thoughtful notes instead. Your written words will lend comfort while respecting the privacy of the patient.

PETIQUETTE: YOUR ANNOYING PETS

You might think your miniature schnauzer with the yappy bark and frou-frou sweater is the sweetest little schnoogums in the world! But beware exhibiting the fatal flaw of excessive pride—also known as pet hubris.

It's just not appropriate, or cute, to speak for your pet on answering machine messages ("Pooky can't come to the phone right now . . ."), or bring him uninvited to visit your friends ("Pooky couldn't wait to say, 'Happy Birthday!'").

As difficult as it may be to conceive, some people don't watch *Animal Planet*. And others are deathly allergic to pet dander, fleas, and drool. For their sake, keep pets at a safe distance when welcoming guests in your home, and exercise moderation while sharing stories about your pet tarantula or iguana. Make sure you ask first before bringing your animal "best friends" with you to visit your other friends. You are free to love whomever you choose; just keep the details to yourself.

RAGE: AAAARGH!

Rage—it's all the rage these days.

When someone cuts you off on the highway? Road Rage. When the wind blows your neighbor's leaves onto your property? Leaf Rage. When a telemarketer interrupts your dinner? Phone Solicitation Rage.

Rage, as in violent fits, or losing control in a violent or angry manner, is never really in style, even though it may be the latest buzz word. Your "Mall Rage" or "Pizza Delivery Guy Rage" is your way of saying, "I can't cope with life's frustrations. I need professional help."

If you should happen to encounter someone acting violently or irrationally (with the exception of, say, presidents or circus clowns), then avoid confrontation and stay out of harm's way. People get downright dangerous when they lose control, so offer up your handkerchief only after the dust settles.

And should you find yourself at the breaking point, call someone who cares—like your personal physician or psychotherapist. Have the good sense to get the help you need, before your Saran Wrap Rage becomes anyone else's business but your own.

SPORTSMANSHIP: TAKE ME OUT AT THE BALL GAME

Two, four, six, eight, how much can sports deteriorate? All the way! All the way! Yeah!

The playing field has gotten mighty ugly these days. No matter the venue, the playback footage is always the same: drunken slobs with painted bellies mooning the camera; athletes brawling with athletes; fans brawling with fans; athletes brawling with fans. And that's just at Little League baseball games.

Elsewhere, cell phones ring on tennis courts and disruptive fans shriek, "You da man!" at the very moment golfers begin their swings.

 What happened to sportsmanship? Where are the humble winners and gracious losers? Since when did boorish, violent, and utterly ridiculous behavior translate into team spirit? Poo yah!

In many ways, sports strip people naked and force them to fight—but not *literally*. Whether you're an athlete or a fan, find ways to ride the waves of victory and defeat with some sense of decorum. And when you do, the cheers (not jeers) will be directed at you.

*Pointers
for Parent Coaches
and Spectators*

- *Model the type of respectful behavior you expect from your child toward referees, umpires, coaches, opposing teams, and other spectators.*

- *Cheer with enthusiasm for the entire team, not just for your child.*

- *Let the coach be the coach. Refrain from publicly scolding or correcting your child during the big game. Just be the supportive parent your child needs— win or lose.*

restaurants

*Spread the table and
contention will cease.*

ENGLISH PROVERB

FOUR STAR RESTAURANT ETIQUETTE

Jumpin' jackrabbits! This place sure is fancy.

Dining out gets tricky for three main reasons: too many servers (valets, coat checkers, maître d's, wine stewards, waiters, and bus boys); too much silverware; and, too much mystery (exotic menu items or menus without prices).

Knowing what's expected of you in a nice restaurant can keep you smiling from escargot through brandied pears. But the most important lessons will help you wherever you may dine.

 By far the biggest breach of restaurant etiquette is rudeness. When you treat waitstaff with condescension or disrespect— even in light of poor service—

you show yourself to be much less superior than you think.

As a general rule, you should not do anything at a restaurant table that you wouldn't do at your dining room table at home (e.g., comb hair, floss teeth, apply make-up). And if you don't understand the menu, by all means ask your friendly waiter to give you a clue.

Other important tips
for dining out include
the following:

- *Find your bread plate to the left, meal plate to the center, and water glass to the right. (Read more about Table Manners on pages 134-43.)*

- *Use silverware from the outside in (e.g., left-to-right on the left; right-to-left on the right).*

- *Keep feet, elbows, and cell phones off the table.*

- *Use eye contact and a raised hand to get the attention of waitstaff.*

- *Respect your waitstaff and fellow diners by not waffling over menu items, or requesting a separate check after ordering drinks.*

Bon appétit!

Restaurant Do's
for the Polite Diner

- Do treat waitstaff with courtesy and respect.

- Do make a reservation, and call to cancel it if necessary.

- Do check personal items when possible, and place purses out of the way of waitstaff or food.

- Do approach your table in this order: first maître d'; then women; then men.

- Do seat guests of honor facing the room or some scenic vista (not the wall), and always to the right of the person picking up the tab.

- Do take a new plate when you make successive trips to a buffet.

- Do keep children from running free or walking about unsupervised.

MONSIEUR, THERE'S A FLY IN MY WINE

Ordering wine in a restaurant can be downright intimidating, and if you're like most people, you reserve the honor for someone else. But when *you* have been deemed the table expert, a few simple tips can carry you through the task of selecting a wine and ceremoniously receiving it.

Wine stewards or sommeliers can make your job easier by suggesting wines that suit your tastes and your dinner. In their absence, at the very least know this: white wines go well with "whiter" foods, such as chicken, pork, or mild-tasting fish; red wines should accompany stronger-tasting foods like smoked, stewed, or grilled meats and fishier fish.

Nod when presented with your bottle of wine (provided the label is correct), and do three things when offered a taste: observe the wine's color (whites should generally be clear, reds may be cloudy but not brown); sniff to detect any "off" odors; and sip to detect any "off" flavors. You may also swirl the wine in your glass to release its bouquet; just don't swirl it all over the tablecloth.

In the rare event that the wine is "corked" (spoiled) and not suitable for drinking, inform the waiter or sommelier, and he should replace the bottle.

But as with food, not liking the wine you selected is not a sufficient reason for sending it back. Live and learn, and order another wine if need be.

A common breach of etiquette and source of hard feelings occurs when drinkers in a group party assume nondrinkers will pay an equal share of the bar tab. Drinkers should avoid this snafu by paying, or at least offering to pay, for their own indulgences.

Tipping: Mathematics for Group Diners

 If the restaurant bill totals $150, how much should each person pay, including tip, if there are five people at the table but only four are paying the bill?

Give up? Ok, here's what you do.

Figure Out the Tip: Tips customarily fall between 15-20% or more of the total bill, excluding the tax. Do not leave a tip less than 15% unless the service was so incredibly atrocious that you need to close your eyes, breathe deeply, and visualize the ocean. In this case, the service was excellent.

Subtract the Tax from the Total Bill: $150 (total bill) - $10 (approximate tax) = $140.

TAKE 20% OF THE SUBTOTAL:
$140 x .20 = $28 (tip for the server)

ADD UP THE BILL TOTAL: Now that you know you need to leave a $28 tip, do some simple arithmetic:

$150 (total bill including tax) + $28 (tip) = $178 (final bill total)

DIVIDE BY THE NUMBER OF CONTRIBUTORS: Since four people will be sharing the bill, then do some simple division:

$178 ÷ 4 = $44. 50 (amount owed by each contributor)

Excellent work: A+

More Tips for Tippers

- Group diners should split the bill when possible; however, if you know you won't be eating dinner when everyone else will, let them know ahead of time and request a separate check.

- Extend holiday tips to people who provide personal services for you throughout the year: hairdressers ($20 or more, or personal gift); mail carriers (restricted by law to $20 or less); newspaper deliverers ($10-20); nanny or au pair (one week's pay or more, plus personal gift from your child); teacher (gift certificate worth $10 or more, and/or personal gift from your child); housekeeper (one day's pay or more); trash/recycling collectors ($10 each or more); building personnel ($10 each or more).

- Tip valets between $1-5, sky caps $1-2 per bag, and concierges $5-10 for each assisted service.

table manners

*Manners are a sensitive awareness of
the feelings of others. If you have that
awareness, you have good manners,
no matter what fork you use.*

Emily Post

TABLING YOUR MANNERS

The dinner table has become a free-for-all these days, and the Lord of the Napkin Rings just stuck chewed gum on his plate. But before you double-dip your roast *orc* in the fondue, take a look around you: *this* is not Middle-Earth. And *that* is not your water glass.

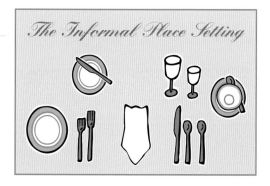

The Informal Place Setting

The first step to deciphering the individual place setting involves locating your drinking glass. While you should always "drink right," as in not gulping or slurping beverages, you should remember that your drink is on the right side of your plate. If you need a status symbol to boost your confidence, think of your BMW while you dine: Bread plate to the left; Meal plate in the center; Water glass to the right.

Use silverware from the outside in, and in the order it is presented (e.g., soup spoon on the outer right, small fork on the far left).

You have two choices when it comes to handling your fork and knife: American-style and European-style. When cutting meat, for example, both Americans and Europeans hold the fork in the left hand, tines down, and the knife in the right hand, blade down. After slicing meat into bite-sized pieces, how-ever, Americans place the knife on the plate (preferably at a diagonal across the upper right side), and switch the fork to the right hand before eating. Europeans hold the fork, tines down, in the left hand while cutting and eating. Either style is correct.

Table Dos

Do place your napkin in your lap, and use it to blot your lips and wipe your hands.

Do wait for your hostess to be seated before you start eating, unless requested to do so earlier.

Do cut food into manageable, bite-sized pieces, and swallow before you speak.

Do say, "Please pass the . . ." instead of reaching across the table and igniting yourself on an open flame.

Do place fork and knife diagonally across the upper right hand corner of your plate when you are finished eating.

Do remove hot or inedible substances from your mouth with your fork, not your fingers or napkin.

Do eat drink garnishes after draining your glass, not before.

Do use a fork when sopping up gravy or sauces with chunks of bread.

Do use finger bowls to clean fingers, and hot towels to clean hands and mouths.

Do refrain from making or receiving phone calls at the table.

Table Don'ts

Don't grasp eating utensils as you would a garden trowel or hammer, or place used utensils directly on the table.

Don't tuck your napkin into your shirt collar.

Don't primp or clean your teeth at the table.

Don't fidget or make loud noises while you eat (e.g., slurping, burping, lip-smacking).

Don't slouch or otherwise lean on the table.

Don't scoop ice from your water glass to cool hot soups or beverages.

Don't season your food before you taste it.

Don't push your plate away from you when you are finished eating.

Don't leave your spoon in your mug while drinking from it, or wring tea bags with your fingers.

Don't dunk donuts or scones into beverages.

Proper Placement of Utensils during a Meal

or

Proper Placement of Utensils after a Meal

PERPLEXING FOODSTUFFS

ARTICHOKES: Pluck off artichoke leaves and scrape the tender part (not the prickly point) between teeth, preferably after dipping in melted butter. Work your way to the delicate inner leaves, then use a knife to cut off the remaining small leaves and feathery innards. Cut the artichoke "heart" into bite-sized pieces and eat with a fork.

ASPARAGUS: Eat asparagus with fingers if served raw as crudités; eat with fork and knife if served with dinner.

BREAD: Break bread into bite-sized pieces,  and butter it or dip it into olive oil one piece at a time.

CRAB (SOFT-SHELLED): Eat entire crab, including shell, either in sandwich form or using a fork and knife. Remove inedibles from your mouth with a fork.

FAJITAS: Place meats, vegetables, and other fillings on flat tortilla. Roll up and use fingers to eat fajita from one end.

FONDUE: Spear bread, vegetables, or fruit with fondue spear and dip into cheese or sauce. Remove food from spear using a dinner fork, and eat from a plate. Do not double dip. Spear uncooked meat cubes and place spear into fondue broth or sauce. When cooked, transfer meat to a plate using a dinner fork and cut into smaller pieces to eat.

LOBSTER: Wear a lobster bib to avoid fishy splatters. Crack shells with shellfish crackers and extract meat with a small fork or pick. Cut larger pieces with a knife, and eat with a fork after dipping in melted butter. Clean your hands by dipping fingers into finger bowls, and use lemon (if provided) to cut extra grease. Dry your hands with your napkin.

PEAS: Use a knife to push peas onto a fork. Do not mash peas before eating, or eat peas from a knife.

RAW SHELLFISH: Use a small fork to extract mussels, clams, or oysters from the half-shell. Season with fresh lemon or cocktail sauce. In informal settings, you may quietly slurp shellfish from shells.

SOUP: Using a soup spoon, spoon soup away from your body and then quietly sip from side of spoon. Tilt bowl away from you to spoon up remaining drops.

SPAGHETTI: Twirl pasta with fork tines into bite-sized portions, and allow any dangling pieces to fall back onto your fork. You may also rest fork tines against the bowl of a spoon while you twirl pasta.

STEAMERS: Extract clam from shell using a

small fork, and use a fork and knife to remove inedible neck. In informal settings, it is permissible to use fingers.

DRINKING FROM BOTTLES, CANS, AND BROWN PAPER BAGS

For as long as beverages have been available in disposable containers, etiquette books have advised people not to drink out of cartons, bottles, and cans. The only exception to this rule was the consumption of beer and soda at outdoor picnics or barbecues, where suitable glasses might not be available.

Nowadays, however, you can buy everything from green tea to chocolate soy milk in packages made from glass, plastic, paper, and  aluminum—or combinations thereof. Convenient little juice boxes come with their own plastic straws, and sports drinks come in wide-mouth containers for easy gulping. People even wear water bottles with designer labels like handbags as they traipse through the mall.

Drinking directly from bottles or cans might be the most convenient option on the tennis court or on the go, but when it comes to serving beverages in your home, drinks should be drunk from a glass, never a can or bottle. And definitely not from the milk carton.

travel

*A traveler of taste will notice that
the wise are polite all over the world,
but the fool only at home.*

OLIVER GOLDSMITH

TOTO, WE'RE NOT IN KANSAS ANYMORE

We live in a global society, a veritable fondue pot of different cultures melting together into one gooey mess. And though we're all simmering in the same pot, we retain very distinct flavors and characteristics linked to our regional and cultural backgrounds.

Proper etiquette in one culture may be a serious breach in another. Gestures such as thumbs up or the OK sign have vulgar connotations elsewhere in the world. Even here at home, people hold differing views of proper etiquette in terms of dress, physical contact, and personal space, to name a few. Tensions flare when people unknowingly disrespect the values and customs of their neighbors.

Before you react to some perceived breach of etiquette, remember that open minds open doors, and the more we seek to understand cultures different from our own, the better we can empathize and forgive.

WHEN PUBLIC TRANSPORTATION GETS PERSONAL

When it comes to public transportation, we have met the enemy. And he is us.

In every sense of the word, he *flies* in the face of proper etiquette—cutting lines, exceeding luggage limitations, and reading from other people's laptops. When he's not adjusting his seat or making loud cell phone calls, he's ranting about scheduling delays, lost luggage, and how the Yankees got robbed in 2004.

And then he multiplies. His wife uses empty seats and seat-back food trays as diaper changing stations for baby. She talks non-stop from New York to L.A. about religion, politics, and how kegel exercises saved her marriage.

What is it about traveling that makes people forget the good manners that apply everywhere else? Is it the combination of cramped leg space and fuel fumes? Some form of motion sickness? You won't let your good manners depart when you do, will you?

uncommon courtesies

The small courtesies sweeten life;
the greater ennoble it.

CHRISTIAN NESTELL BOVEE

RSVP:
OH NO YOU *DIDN'T!*

We have no trouble reading invitations that request our presence at social or business functions. Costume party? Great—I'll be Snoop Dog! Conference in Hawaii? *Aloooha!*

But we fail miserably when it comes to replying to an RSVP (literally, *répondez s'il vous plaît,* or *please reply lest you be considered terribly rude*). Could it be that we're afraid to commit? Are we so flooded with invitations that we can't find our way to the phone?

Regardless, there's simply no excuse for failing to respond. Party hosts need accurate

 head counts to ensure adequate supplies and happy guests. Do you want to be responsible for (*gasp*) not enough

goody bags at Junior's birthday party, or (*double gasp*) not enough gin at Senior's?

Respect other people's time and thoughtfulness when they send you an invitation. Call them by the appointed date if it says, "Please respond" or "RSVP," and if you cannot attend, call them if it says, "Regrets Only." Whatever you do, just call them. Or next time, there might not be a next time.

PUNCTUALITY: FASHIONABLY ON TIME

Concepts of punctuality vary by culture, but here in the United States, the fashionable time to arrive is usually the time you've agreed to meet. But not always.

Being "on time" to events like cocktail parties or social mixers can mean arriving anywhere from fifteen minutes to an hour plus *after* the appointed starting time. Arriving slightly "late" makes good sense at after-hours parties, but waltz into the bar at the distinctly unhappy hour of 8 o'clock, and you can forget about the free buffet.

Arrive early for doctor's appointments, wedding ceremonies, funerals, and job interviews. A window of about fifteen minutes gives you ample time to complete paperwork or otherwise get where you need to be. Of course, you must allow for extra time when flying commercially or utilizing public transportation.

Most other special occasions are relatively straightforward. If the invitation says, "Surprise Party at 7 o'clock," don't show up at 8 o'clock. But don't arrive early, either, particularly for dinner parties or kids' birthday parties. Reading the invitation is always your best bet.

NOISE POLLUTION: EXCUSE ME, I BELIEVE THUMPING IS WRONG WITH YOUR CAR

There's a rush on ear plugs in aisle six, and here's why: movie theater speakers, Fourth of July fireworks displays, car stereos cranked up so high that vibrations can be felt by people three cars away, obnoxious cell phone ring tones.

Bursting your neighbor's ear drums is just plain *bad manners*. Safely assume that no one wants to hear your lawnmower at 10:00 PM or your dog barking till dawn.

Always think twice before doing or saying anything within earshot of others—and especially before you belch or break up with your boyfriend from your cubicle at work.

And for the sake of all that is good and proper, turn off your cell phone when at weddings and funerals, and pump down the volume everywhere else.

zero tolerance

*A bad manner spoils everything, even reason
and justice; a good one supplies everything,
gilds a No, sweetens a truth, and adds
a touch of beauty to old age itself.*

BALTASAR GRACIÀN

JUST SAY "NO THANK YOU" TO BAD MANNERS

People show an appalling lack of decorum when they think no one is looking. If they're not adjusting undergarments or picking noses, they're parking in handicapped spots and cutting lines.

But even when they know they're being watched, they brazenly run stop signs, bark into cell phones, and show condescension and disrespect to people who get in their way—cashiers, receptionists, the elderly.

One of the fundamental rules of etiquette—and world peace, for that matter—is treating others as you would like to be treated yourself. The Golden Rule. That's the easy part, and by far most people *do* treat others with kindness, consideration, and respect.

When confronted by someone else's atrocious behavior, however, sometimes we snap. We jump right off the etiquette boat and sink to the level of the offender. Unfortunately for us, this lack of restraint reflects poorly on our own manners.

The time to exercise the very best behavior is exactly when others show their worst. Be the calm while others storm, the peace while others rage—without shaking your head or tsk-tsking a finger. Good manners will triumph in the end. They always do.

The End